Contents

Acknowledgments:

First, let me thank God for guiding and watching over my life.

I would like to give a huge thank you to Stephney Riley, my mother/best friend/COO for not only giving me life but always speaking greatness over my life since birth.

Thank you to my dad, Erik Thomas, for always leading by example and for the life lessons I still carry to this day. Shoutout and much love to Triss, Mimi, and Janness.

Thank you to Nana, Papa, Aunt Donna, Aunt Erin, Uncle Cadell/Aunt Ginger, and the rest of the Thomas Family for putting that hustle and relentlessness in me.

Thank you to the Riley family for instilling love, care, and compassion in me.

Shoutout to all my friends that I consider family. I truly love y'all and appreciate the support. Special shoutout to Myles Moss; blood couldn't make us any closer.

Shoutout to "MR. MAKE A PLAY", aka Remy G. I couldn't ask for a better co-host of FYI FLI The Podcast, Chief Marketing Officer of FYI FLI, or even a better friend.

Thank you to the good folks at RMMFI for accepting me as their first out-of-state applicant to their business program. I learned so much and met many amazing people; Romales, Monique, Jeremy, Martin, Douglas, and other classmates.

Thank you to Maryville College, especially Dr. Gallagher, Mr. Timmy, Twitch, Anne and Aimee, The Bonner Scholar Program, Coach Hayes, and Coach Cart.

Special thank you to my mentors, Johnny C. Taylor, Jr., and the rest of the FYI FLI advisory board: Luke Hohmann, Adam Sohn, Emilio Pineda, and Lisa Freberg.

A big thank you to my FYI FLI Team Day Ones: Lauren Long and Jennifer Colter. And this could not be possible without my editors, Martha Frase and Audrey Riley, and graphic designer, Sam Segal.

Introduction

This book really began in the fall of 2019. I was a college senior playing running back after switching from playing safety my first three years at Maryville College in Tennessee. It was just the fifth week of the season, and my head coach let me know that the game against our rival, Huntington, was my chance to start if I did well in practice. There were four other running backs ahead of me, but none were producing as needed.

Keep in mind; I hadn't played running back since my sophomore year of high school in 2014. I had raw talent and ability, but what I lacked was patience. My coach worked on this with me, and by week two of the season, it clicked!

Honestly, I compared it to the EA Sports Madden Football Game. On the newer Madden video games, you can't just hold the sprint button down the whole time. You have to be strategic when you accelerate and burst through an open hole, and that's what I did. I used my coach's tips and my Madden gameplay to fine-tune my running back skills, and boy did it start paying off. By the second week of the season, I began tearing them boys up in practice, breaking long run after long run. It was finally my time to shine.

I began week five going with the starters, just as my coach promised. I was confident and excited to finally get the shot I felt I deserved. And then...BOOM! We do a simple running play in practice, not going too hard to preserve ourselves for Saturday's game against our rival. The defense wraps me up but doesn't let me fall to the ground, and while I'm standing, my teammate blocks another player to the ground. Unfortunately, there was something between my falling teammate and the ground. That something was my KNEE!

I immediately shouted something my mama would never want to hear me say and attempted to stretch it out. Knowing that this was my first opportunity to start at running back, I tried to push through and keep playing, but the pain was too much. I limped to the sideline and began stretching some more, and then I heard a very loud POP! At this point, I could put zero weight on my right leg. I hopped over to my coach and told him repeatedly, "I'm done...I'm done..."

I had torn my meniscus. My football season was over, forever.

This was a very tough and difficult situation to go through, considering this was my last year of playing college football. Looking back at it in my rearview mirror,

that injury was a blessing in disguise. That injury propelled me to turn my energy and attention to writing my senior research paper.

I had chosen the topic of financial literacy for students and young adults because, looking around, I noticed the lack of financial education coming from my peers. I graduated with a major in business management and a minor in marketing, so I'd taken many classes dealing with money. I felt like I had an above-average knowledge of money, but what about my peers in the art, communications, criminal justice, and all the other majors that don't require any type of business or finance class? If they weren't taught at home, then how could we expect our youth to graduate financially prepared for "adulting".

I realized just how much good information and insights I was collecting and thought it deserved a larger audience hungry for this kind of knowledge that just wasn't available in the K-12 or even college basic curriculum. I thought it would make a great book or guide for young people who want to take better control over their financial lives. It was my cousin, Myles, who encouraged me to turn my research paper into a mobile app instead of a book.

Well, I'm the type of person that, when I hear a great idea, I'm going to turn that **idea** into **action**. So, from September to December 2019, I did nothing but research, research, research.

After having my surgery in December, I told my mom that when I got back to campus, I was going to meet with faculty and staff until I worked my way up to the Dean of Students, and that's exactly what I did.

After hopping around on crutches to over 15+ meetings, I secured my meeting for March 3rd, 2020, with Dean Klingensmith, my business professor, Dr. Gallagher, and four other prominent faculty members. I presented the collection of financial literacy resources I hoped to turn into an app for young people. This meeting went incredibly well, and there is one reason why.

Preparation. I literally began preparing three weeks prior to the meeting and for the first time in my life, I felt overprepared. Now there really is no such thing as being over-prepared, but I wanted to emphasize how hard I worked to get ready and how much time I dedicated to that one moment. **Proper preparation truly does prevent poor performance!** My fear of potentially blowing an amazing opportunity to present to the dean of Maryville College propelled me to ensure that I was prepared and ready to knock it out of the park.

After the meeting, I had my mindset on one thing...my last Spring Break! A group of 10 friends and myself found a 10-bed villa on the strip in Las Vegas. We had been planning this trip since November of 2019, and everyone already paid their part for the house and booked flights with no complications.

Then came March 13th; I could never forget that date. That's the day the COVID-19 virus was officially acknowledged as a national threat and President Trump declared a state of National Emergency. In the days following, businesses, schools, and transport started shutting down. My friends and I anxiously watched the news and checked social media to see what was happening in Vegas.

It started with all parties and events canceled, then grocery stores and convenience stores were empty due to panic purchases. Finally, at 11:45 pm on March 15, Vegas announced that they were shutting down casinos and going into full lockdown mode. That night, everyone was blowing up my phone, trying to see what we were going to do. Ultimately, I had to cancel the Airbnb and my flight along with my friends.

The next few days on campus were very strange. Tons of people had already left for spring break while my friends and I were still on campus. A lot of us were from out of state, thousands of miles from home. Eventually, the school made a decision that everyone should leave campus, and we would continue classes online. Such a drastic change of plans for everyone; we thought we were going to be in Vegas turning up, but instead, we were all in shock about what was transpiring right in front of our eyes. The entire world is going on lockdown due to a global pandemic from some kind of virus called COVID-19. I packed up as much stuff as I could and hopped on the road to Chattanooga, Tennessee, to take one of my friends home, and then to Atlanta to drop another friend off at the airport. Now alone, I reflected on the coming months as I drove the eight hours to my father's home in Florida, where I would finish off my senior year...virtually, on a computer screen.

Now let me tell you, this was one of the most challenging ordeals I have faced. You know what "senioritis" is, right? When a high school or college senior doesn't want to do anything but graduate! Well, imagine that times 200!

Not only was I ready to graduate, but what nobody besides my closest friends knew was that since my injury in September, I had been working on building a financial literacy empire. So my mind, body, and spirit were in full entrepreneur mode. Not being in a classroom environment literally made it much harder for me to focus.

I began working for Delivery Dudes (Florida's version of DoorDash) to make some consistent income to put back into the business. That's all I was concerned about— making money and my new baby...I mean business LOL. I muddled through the last month of class and completed my four years in a grand celebratory fashion: Online Zoom Graduation.

My mom can literally tell you this story. She called me at the beginning of the ceremony and said, "Hassan, why didn't you tell me you were graduating today?" My response? "I didn't know—-I've been locked in."

I was so focused on planting the seeds and building the foundation for FYI FLI that I missed my own graduation. This determination was not unrewarded, though. In April 2020, around my birthday, I got a meeting with the President and CEO of the Society for Human Resource Management in the Washington DC area. Johnny C. Taylor, Jr., a professional colleague of my mother, had recognized the immense potential of the financial literacy brand I was building and introduced me to the President of SHRM India, Ms. Achal Khanna, who connected me with her development team.

This team of developers and I got off to a great start. That is until COVID went into full swing over there, and all communications between myself and the developers in India ceased for a month and a half.

When they finally reached back out, I learned someone on their team had caught the virus. Now it was early August, and my website was supposed to be completed by the end of the month and the app a couple of months later. Nevertheless, when God says no to one thing, he always says yes to another!

I was determined to keep my momentum going on this new business I was launching. **I called it FYI FLI: For Your Information Financial Literacy & Investing.** It wasn't my plan to target the traditional customers of financial advice—people with money to spend and invest. I wanted to help bridge the gap between education and entertainment for young Millennials and Gen Z'ers who are struggling with small incomes, student debt, and poor credit, who are perhaps trying to break out of generational poverty that may be plaguing their family and community.

I decided my next move was to start a financial literacy podcast.

Starting a podcast from scratch turned out to be no easy feat, but it is something I will never regret.

Probably the most interesting part of creating the podcast was bringing all the material together for my audience of young Millennials and Gen Z. The process allowed me to interject myself into the financial literacy community and talk to influential and creditable entrepreneurs and educators in their respective fields.

I honestly believe that's what a podcast could do for you as well!
**Every influencer, business owner, and even athlete should
have a podcast.** By getting out of your comfort zone and voicing
your opinions, others will begin to trust you and value your
expertise. Once you acquire that mantle of trust and credibility, you
can now monetize any and all offerings you can create.

Another reason starting a podcast was clutch for me and could do
wonders for you is the **value exchange**. I'll touch on this more later,
but the value exchange of a podcast is a key factor when speaking
to potential sponsors, guests, and business partners.

Podcasting is a relatively new media, but it has already taken over
streaming media, both audio and video.

Business leaders and entrepreneurs understand that podcasts are
the new way for people to digest information, and the value of your
podcast is that it's a vessel for information that a business wants to
relay to its potential customers.

This value exchange is how I was able to secure some of my most
influential guests in our first season, including the actress and
comedian GloZell; NFL player and owner of Sweet Ventures LLC,
William Sweet, and many other big-time business owners. They all
have a story to tell, and I have a podcast where people will listen to
an interesting and impactful story. Since August 2020, the podcast
has had over 15,000 downloads by listeners in 40-plus countries.

I also began teaching financial literacy classes online, and have
conducted more than 20 so far, bringing this key information to
individuals ranging in age from 5 to 60. Then we also secured our
business foundation with a company called Centsai.

Their support is allowing us to pair FYI FLI's diverse and relatable
content with a certified national curriculum that we can take to high
schools and colleges. Our ambition is to implement our financial
curriculum into every high school, college, and trade school in the

world, because money is a global language that everyone wants to speak—fluently!

My Lockdown Lessons

While this was going on, the world was in various stages of lockdown, masking, and social distancing. Most people lost income, friends, family, and some even lost momentum in fulfilling their dreams. Not the best environment to be starting a new business, but it was definitely a jumpstart for learning.

I want to share the five biggest lessons I learned during the 2020-2021 COVID-19 pandemic.

1. Providing value is essential, but it's not number 1. **Number 1 is to Keep God First.**

As entrepreneurs, we often feel like we are self-made and that we are the ones making everything happen. But without God's grace, we are nothing. He is the one who chooses to bless us, but please don't think it's all just by faith.

James 2:14-26 says, "Faith without works is dead." Now, what does that mean? It means that simply believing in God is not enough; we must actively pursue his love and our dreams to be blessed in abundance.

Life is all about **balance** and **priorities**. During the pandemic, with churches and synagogues unable to have in-person services, some switched to virtual services. After some research to learn if any churches had podcasts, I found a couple that I really liked. One podcast that stood out was "The Transformation Church" by Pastor Mike Todd and a couple of other incredible preachers.

This church's energy and relatable message made it a clear winner for me, but there are no losers—whoever is praising God and spreading the gospel has already won!

I am telling you this as an example of how you can add balance to your life. Even in lockdown, we don't have to sit around and listen to our favorite rappers or stream content all day. **We must balance our education and entertainment intake.**

It's okay to make small incremental changes. Nothing's wrong with listening to Drake and Roddy Rich 60% of the time educational/self-improvement podcasts 20%, and religion-based content 20%. You are balanced. I came to realize that whatever you listen to or feed your spirit with, you actually begin to mimic that. With that being said, let's make sure we are allowing a mixture of positive and enjoyable things into our spirit.

Keeping God first was a critical component for my success. For you, that may mean keeping some form of belief in a higher power. As we were all impacted by Covid, we needed to have a spiritual force to believe in when it seems like the world is against us and nothing is right.

2. **Providing Value** comes in at a strong number two. Whenever and whatever room you enter, you must do three things: show up, show out, and provide value! That goes for bricks and mortar rooms as well as Zoom meeting rooms.

Those three things will assure you are remembered in a room with a bunch of big dogs and heavy hitters. We must be able to analyze everyone else's strengths and weaknesses, and once we do that, we must fill their weak cup from our strong cup.

While I was in Atlanta for Earn Your Leisure's first InvestFest networking event, I felt that I had a lot to offer. Most of the attendees at the event were entrepreneurs, not podcasters. So, with that in mind, the smart move for me was to offer value to these entrepreneurs who did not already have a specified platform by providing them with just that—a place to tell their story and promote their brand at a time when podcasts were filling a huge void in people's locked-down lives.

Remember, value is something you exchange. So, now the entrepreneurs could provide me and my audience with valuable content based on real experiences from real people. Our audience would normally have to pay for this content in a coaching session, course, or expensive mastermind class. **So, the moral of the story: lead with value, and all your relationships will be meaningful.**

But here's a warning–don't ever be naive and let people take advantage of you. When someone shows you their true actions and intent, believe them!

3. The third lesson is huge. **Eliminate all distractions and negativity,** including people.

Let's just stop and think about how much time we have wasted on people who were not worth it. It's probably a lot, yes I know. I'm glad you're reading this book, though, because, after this, they're going to think your name was K Camp the way you cut everyone off! LOL, I'm kidding... not everyone, but those people who are slowing you down from accomplishing your mission have to go! And you don't need to feel bad about it either!

We have only one life, and I know you're one of those people who put everyone else before yourself. But your business is the child that you chose to bring into this world. Everything and everyone who isn't for the good of that child needs to be put aside.

At the same time, you are taking care of your business, take care of yourself. **You have to make sure you are doing okay physically, mentally, and fiscally** before you can care for your business. At the end of the day, you are the one who has to deal with the rewards and consequences of every single choice you make, so why not make the choices that will yield the highest ROI for you?

After graduating and leaving college, I went through my Snapchat list, Instagram, and basically all my social media and unfollowed and distanced myself from people who never supported my company or me. These people are just taking up mental space and energy, especially because some of them were people I grew up with and who I expected to show nothing but love, as I always have.

This brings me back to **my mom's advice, which is to focus on your supporters and watch them grow!** This idea changed my life and allowed me to basically develop tunnel vision. I only give my time and energy to things that I have placed in my tunnel, like God, family, and FYI FLI. Other than that, I'm pretty much locked in.

4. **Live in reality.** This is a message for the ages because many of us choose to have a false sense of reality. Everything's okay, or it's not that bad. Just so we don't have to be the person to address the problem or the person to come up with a solution.

Whether it be a false sense of reality about an addiction, weight loss/gain, appearance, a significant other, or even business, **we must do one of the hardest things; to be honest with ourselves.** It is incredibly hard, and it's something you have to force yourself to do because of the results and the progression that will come from this self-honesty and awareness.

The first step in solving a problem is actually understanding the problem. So, If I can get you to believe in yourself enough to acknowledge and tackle the problems in your life, we have won. Remember this: **we must turn anger into action.** That's the only way to get over any negative thing that occurs in your life. Gotta make a plan and make a play! Simple as that.

For example, COVID-19 gave everyone in the world an unheard-of opportunity. We had the chance to be in our homes for over a year. The world that normally moves at a fast and relentless pace, slowed down and suddenly became still. This historical and unprecedented time could have been used in a multitude of ways. Whether you used that time to self pity or self improve, this book will equip you with lessons and tips to increase productivity that will boost your confidence and execution skills. We will not harp on what you did or didn't do in the past. What matters is your mindset and outlook on the future and how you plan on improving each day.

> 5. Last major lesson learned during Covid was
>   to **embrace fear.**

After graduating from college to COVID, I jumped headfirst into starting a business. I had my first newspaper interview, my first radio interview, and taught my first webinar, all within the first two months of graduating college. Was I nervous? Heck yeah, I was! But what kept me from being so nervous that I couldn't perform was my preparation.

It is a true saying that proper preparation prevents poor performance. That preparation allows me to go into these classes I teach and different speaking engagements with confidence because I know I put the work into shine, and I deserve it.

That's another thing—**you deserve it! Please don't have survivor's remorse.** If you don't know what that is, it's feelings of guilt because you were the one who made it out to strive toward your goals and success.

Yes, you and all your friends came from the same place, but did they put in the same amount of work as you? Did they make the same amount of sacrifices you had to make? God's blessings for you are for you and no one else. So please do not question God or the work you've put in.

Look fear in its face, accept it, and do it anyway! Accept and embrace the risk and do it anyway!

These lessons are what I've taken from a tough situation and turned into a blossoming business.

That's the central purpose of the FYI FLI podcast. Over the past year, I have been privileged to speak with successful business builders and learn their secrets. And now it's my pleasure to share their insights with you and what I learned from them along the way.

Chapter 1: Belief In A Higher Power
Byron Sellers
Co-founder, Mobile Home Elite Investors

Known as the Mobile Home Millionaire, this guy is a very intelligent, humble, and down-to-earth dude. In 2018, he started his elite mobile home empire with his wife and queen Sharnice. During our interview, I asked what the biggest lesson he's learned from COVID-19 is, and he said, **"Belief in a higher power."**

This is very important because we all can burn out. We are human. Going through that year of quarantine, the days seemed as if they were repeating themselves—as if it was the Twilight Zone. So, burnout, exhaustion, frustration, depression were to be expected.

We have never gone through a time like this one! And that's why believing in a higher power should be a priority. **Faith** can give us that spark—that boost that we need to continue going. That belief that we need to push through a hard time like COVID-19 or whatever we may face in life. Like I learned myself, gotta keep God first!

One of Byron's quotes that really stuck with me was, **"Monetize your genius."** When I heard this quote from Byron Sellers, I was like, "Oweeeee, that goes hard!" This quote literally sums up the way to profit off yourself in this world we live in today!

Jay-Z's famous quote, **"I'm not a businessman, I'm a business man,"** can apply to everyone, man or woman. This is exactly what Byron Sellers and his queen did. They packaged up their knowledge from three years of killing it in the mobile home game into an online course teaching students how to invest in mobile homes like traditional real estate. The sellers used Thinkfic to start selling (no pun intended) their courses, and in under a year, they retailed over $1 million worth of courses! You can say the sellers were sellin' (pun intended!)

So, what made Byron and Sharnice so special? They were not afraid. They jumped out of their comfort zone and created a digestible and valuable course for their audience. This is the same thing YOU can do with whatever skill you have.

We live in an information-driven world. So, whatever you are talented at or can do easily, why not package that information up as an **E-course, E-book, podcast, or other learning product and start bringing in passive income!** With the technology and resources available to us, it has never been easier to monetize yourself and bring in money while you sleep. Who doesn't want money pouring in while you sleep? Exactly! The value of creating a digital product is that you create it one time. Put your head down, lock-in, and grind. Knock out your product and then sell it over and over again for the rest of your life!

These types of assets are so valuable to people because we live in an information-hungry world—people are on YouTube all day watching and learning how to do things. They are actively searching for someone or some business credible enough to teach them how to do something. Why not let that SOMEONE be YOU. Let's get active!

Another major lesson was understanding the importance of a **mindset shift** when trying to change your life around.

A mindset shift is setting your mind to perform to your best ability! This quote is critical because no major transformation can happen in your life without a mindset shift.

Have you ever heard the saying, "You can't help someone who doesn't want to be helped?" Well, do you know why? Because their mindset is locked in their old ways, and until they are able to shift their mind to want to perform at their best ability, they never will! You should never make a move unless your mind and heart are 100% in it! We FYI FLI folks don't half step—we are big steppers!

Key Takeaways:
- Believe in a higher power.
- Monetize your genius
- Mindset Shift

Chapter 2: Locked In
Ralph Jarvis, Jr.
Income Strategist and Business Coach

Coming out of Philly—my brother, mentor, and fellow bag chaser, Ralph Jarvis, Jr., he's a true go-getter.

From his digital marketing and advertising game to website development, all the way to his rideshare rental car play, Ralph means biz! The lesson he learned from COVID is to **"stay locked in"** or to stay focused on your **purpose** and **passion**.

This was a powerful message to hear because hundreds and even thousands of negative matters cross our path every day, but the only way to bypass them and keep striving for greatness is to stay locked in! This goes back to what my college football coach used to say, **"Control the controllables."**

Although Ralph dropped plenty of thought-provoking and action-activating gems on our show, there was one topic I wanted to focus on. It's the rental car play that has shot Ralph to a whole new level.

Basically, there are two main rideshare platforms that most people use, and they operate similarly to Airbnb. The Hyrecar platform is more often used by people who want to make some extra money driving Uber or Lyft using someone else's vehicle. The Turo platform, which is where Ralph focuses, is used more by everyday renters on vacation. As I like to explain them to people, these rideshare platforms are literally just like AIRBNB but for cars. You can rent your car out to others and profit up to $1200 a month!

'But this seems risky; I don't want other people to have my car." No worries! The app's insurance covers the vehicles, so by following the proper procedures, you can eliminate most of the risk.

The first time Ralph and I spoke, he wasn't yet heavily invested in the rideshare rental game, but as of now, our guy has four cars in his Turo lineup and an E-course to show others how to profit.

The course shows how to generate passive income by setting up systems and processes to have you making money while you're sleeping.

One of the best benefits of Turo is that it brings in passive income. **"It's cool to have multiple streams of income, but multiple streams of passive income is where it's at!" Ralph told me.** Be sure to tap in with our guy to see how you can turn a liability like a car into an income-generating asset!

Key Takeaways:
• Remain Locked in
• Multiple streams of passive income
• TURO!

Chapter: 3 Lean Info Fear
Cinneah El-Amin, aka Fly.nanced
Product Manager, Personal Finance & Travel Influencer

One of the best lessons Ms. Cinneah El-Amin—known on Instagram as Fly.nanced— learned during COVID was to **"lean into fear."**

She referenced how she wanted to start her company in 2018 but didn't, due to fear of rejection and fear of people calling her a hypocrite because she was still in debt. This is called **Imposter Syndrome**, which is when people doubt themselves and believe that others will expose them as some sort of a fraud.

2020 really gave Cinneah the wind beneath her wings because she realized by taking her leap of faith that people responded to her authenticity—not a perceived "expert" status. You do not have to be perfect to motivate someone else. You don't need to have 10,000 followers to make an impact on someone's life. Be you and understand that is enough!

Think about it like this—**if your goal is to be relatable—just be yourself! No one is perfect, so we can all relate to that!**

Now, travel hacking was something new to me. Being the type of person I am, I have always tried to find ways to have the MOST fun for the least expense, and that's basically what travel hacking is. It's the process of using travel reward points—credit cards, hotels, airline rewards, cash-back sites, etc.—to offset or reduce your cost of traveling.

Cinneah told me that on average, Black Americans spend $600 per domestic leisure stay, based on a 2019 study done by MMGY. Not a trip to Dubai or Hong Kong, but a trip to Atlanta, Miami, L.A.— those types of trips. She and I both agreed that living below your means does not mean not living your life at all! We are not telling you not to travel and see the world—we are telling you to have a plan that will allow you to do so without blowing your whole bag!

One strategy Cinneah offered during our interview was to have a travel fund or a sinking fund. Make a habit of regularly saving into this account through regular transfers or having a part of your paycheck directly deposited into this account. The smart thing to do in creating this fund (which I did after interviewing her) is to open a separate high-yield savings account **(HYSA)**. It's just like a regular savings account, but they give you a higher APY or return on your money than your regular savings account. **So, open up an HYSA and schedule regular automatic transfers to that account. The benefit of doing this is that your money grows without remembering to add or transfer funds into it.**

Well, why is that so good? It's good because when it's time for a vacation, you don't want to be pulling from your bill money, monthly spending money, and you REALLY don't want to be pulling from your regular savings account.

So now you see where a travel fund comes in handy. Two more tips Cinneah shared with us was 1) when traveling, invest in an under-seat bag along with a carry-on, so you don't have to pay baggage fees. And 2) when you buy a ticket with Spirit, Frontier or another budget airline, buy the ticket in-person to save 60 to 100 dollars in online convenience fees! Gem after gem from Cinneah of Flynanced!

Key takeaways:
• Lean into fear
• Travel hacking is the process of using travel reward points to reduce your cost of traveling.
• Invest in an under-seat bag to avoid baggage fees.
• Buy plane tickets in-person to save online convenience fees.

Chapter 4: Life Is Fragile
Lawrence Cain Jr
CEO of Abundance University

Lawrence Cain, Jr., the humble G.O.A.T.

Lawrence was one of the first people I interviewed when I started my podcast. It is easy to tell why he is so widely loved and admired by his peers. Lawrence gives off a genuine, caring, yet solid aura, and I can honestly say he is someone that I try to model myself after.

Lawrence and his company, Abundance University, have several different resources to push financial literacy, like courses, classes, a podcast, and even multiple books! I asked Lawrence what the biggest lesson he learned during COVID was, and he said, **"Life is fragile."**

What Lawrence meant by this is that we must live our lives to the fullest every single day. As we've seen during this pandemic, with people losing their health battles day and night, it's clear that life is not something that should be taken for granted. Every day on this earth is a blessing, and we must treat it that way.

Looking back on my life, I can't remember one day when I didn't get better at something. We must improve our positions every day, which goes back to one of the most important keys in life: **goal setting**. Let's not just aimlessly wander around and go through the motions. Let's set a goal and then **make a plan and make a play, baby!** As for me, I have found that financial literacy is my thing, so any course, podcast, YouTube video, or conference involving financial literacy, FYI FLI and I are there.

Now one of my biggest takeaways from the humble G.O.A.T, as I like to call Lawrence Cain, was the importance of **paying off your debts. "Debt literally robs you of the wealth you are trying to build,"** he said, and I agree with him wholeheartedly

Lots of financial gurus like to use the term **"Pay yourself first,"** but it's really hard to pay yourself first if you have to pay student loans, car loans, and credit card debt. You may ask, but why do I need to pay these loans back to zero when I can just keep making minimum monthly payments? Well, if you don't clear your debt, then it can really hurt your credit score which will make it difficult to buy your first car or house.

Lawrence gave us some amazing tips on paying down debt. His personal favorite was the **"debt avalanche"** method, which is paying off your creditor with the highest amount owed and highest interest rate first to avoid paying more money over time. On the other hand, the **"debt snowball"** method starts with your smallest amounts of debt and knocks those out while paying the minimum on your larger debts. The benefit of this method is that it gives you the mental momentum of paying off debts and working toward larger goals.

Key takeaways:
- Life is fragile
- Set goals
- Pay off debts
- Debt Avalanche Method
- Debt Snowball Method

Chapter 5: Be Resilient
Danielle Shirley
Founder, The Intentional Money University

A special shoutout goes to Mrs. Danielle Shirley, who is a supporter and will surely be a life-long friend. Speaking with Danielle was an amazing experience. Her passion for helping and educating people speaks volumes.

The top lesson she learned during COVID was how **resilient** we as a people could be! We all went from living our comfortable lives to being stuck in our homes (if we were blessed enough to have one) during a worldwide pandemic. Despite those negative things, many of us found ways to make the best of the situation at hand, which is a characteristic we need to keep with us for the rest of our lives.

Sometimes the only option is to play the cards we are dealt. My football coach used to say, "**Control the controllables,**" and this quote speaks volumes. If during COVID-19 you spent time dwelling on not being able to go outside without a mask and other things you could not control, you probably became really miserable. On the other hand, if you showed characteristics of resiliency and followed my old coach's quote, you should have been able to come out of quarantine with a new skill, hobby, interest, or another positive attribute that you can build on in the future.

As far as the biggest takeaways from our interview: I learned from Danielle to be **intentional** with my money. Your intention should be seen in your financial habits, your social interactions, your relationships—everywhere. Being intentional is so important because you know and everyone around you knows exactly what you're focused on.

That's one thing I can relate to very closely because, during the pandemic, I really became intentional in developing **tunnel vision** on things that were important to me. If you didn't make the list of people or things I cared about, you didn't receive my energy.

Our energy is worth protecting. If we spend time and energy on someone or something that provides us no positive benefit or feeling, what are we doing? Why are we there? It's literally a waste!

Determine the things and people in your life that you care for and those who also care for you and make sure you go hard for them. Whatever falls outside of that list—let it go! It's time to lock in!

Another huge lesson I learned from Danielle Shirley was, "Don't be a **lifestyle creep**." When she used that unfamiliar term, I had to go back to my middle school days and use my context clues to understand the meaning. She added, **"Just because you get more money doesn't mean you increase your lifestyle expenses."** This is especially important for new college grads and young people starting careers. And it's something I see a lot with my peers! After graduating, we get a new job and have constant money coming in and feel like it's okay to wild out because we know another check is coming in a week or two.

This ain't it! The simplest way to build wealth and not live paycheck to paycheck is to consistently **spend less than you make or make more than you spend.** So, remember, when you get a bigger bag, don't give in to lifestyle creep. Figure out what you need to live on and create a budget that includes saving, investing, and, most importantly, FUN!

Key Takeaways:
- Be resilient
- Control the controllables
- Be intentional
- Don't give in to "lifestyle creep"

Chapter 6: Time-Efficiency
Jawon Merius
CEO and Founder of Equity Tax & Accounting

My guy, 24-year-old entrepreneur out of New Jersey, Mr. Jawon Merius. One of the greatest things about starting a podcast is having the opportunity to connect with like-minded individuals. Coming across this young driven brother, who started his own tax and accounting firm out of college, was nothing short of a blessing!

Speaking of blessings, when I asked Jawon Merius about his biggest takeaway from COVID, Jawon said, "lockdown allowed him to **focus** on building his brand and coming up with systems and processes to run his business more **efficiently**."

This really related to me because when COVID-19 began hitting hard in March and April of 2020, a lot of people were comparing it to the Black Plague. No, people were not dying from the virus at the same rate as the plague, but the similarity is that many entrepreneurs grew their wealth considerably during that time. I truly believe this opportunity will be the same.

Another huge takeaway from Jawon is the importance of **understanding taxes**. Not just as a businessperson but as an American citizen! It blows my mind that even basic tax vocabulary is not taught in school!

If our guardians aren't telling us that a tax deduction lowers your taxable income and a tax credit lowers the amount of taxes you pay, we would never know! If you are not knowledgeable about taxes, you are most likely overpaying. I saw a statistic recently that 71% of people overpay their taxes.

Taxes literally impact every age, occupation, and income bracket. Did you know that college students are eligible for four different tax breaks? The American Opportunity Tax Credit, the Lifetime Learning Credit, the tuition and fees deduction, and the student loan interest deduction.

We also need to understand taxes too when it comes to investing. The government likes to reward people who **buy and hold** (which should be all of us!). They give us this tax break in the form of long-term capital gain tax rates versus short-term capital gains. **So, if you hold an asset for a year or longer, you will be taxed at a max of 20% compared to short-term capital gains tax at a maximum of 37%. So, as you can see, just from being knowledgeable about financial literacy and proper management practices, we can save tons of money! I guess knowledge truly is power!**

Key Takeaways:
- Use your time wisely
- Tax Deduction and Tax Credits
- Four tax breaks for college students.
- Long-term capital gains vs. Short-term capital gains

Chapter 7: Take Action
Dr. Makeba Butler
Digital Business Coach & Entrepreneur

One of my all-time favorite guests! When I first jumped on a Zoom call with Dr. Makeba Butler, she immediately started giving me "Favorite Professor" vibes. Dr. Butler holds multiple degrees: a Master's Degree from Arkansas State University and a Doctorate degree in Transformational Leadership from Concordia University, Portland.

Her greatest lesson learned from going through the COVID-19, and quarantine dilemma we all endured is to **take action**! Dr. Butler said, "During COVID-19, we had people who stood back and observed and people who took action." Take a moment to think about which person you were. If you didn't take action, it's okay because you are reading this book. **The financial and entrepreneurial knowledge you are gaining will help you make a plan and make a play!**

Other important truths from Dr. Butler include the real meaning of **"financial freedom,"** the different methods of achieving it, and the main reasons young folks need to be investing early and often!

To start, everyone's definition of financial freedom is different, but Dr. Butler's, in my opinion, is spot on! When she thinks of financial freedom, **she thinks of "time freedom and option freedom"— as having the time and the options to do whatever you please, whenever you please!**

"Money doesn't make you happy, but money gives you options." If that quote from Dr. Butler doesn't stick, then I don't know what will!

I believe so heavily in promoting financial literacy because it's what will bring true financial freedom to our communities. Because when you don't have money, your options and time are limited and controlled by money or the lack of it! So that is why this lesson is so important.

Dr. Butler gave us four more main areas we need to focus on to become financially free. **Investing, active and passive income, multiple streams of income, and your compounding interest.**

Investing is so important because it's the true way to build **generational wealth**. The stock market has generated an average return between **7-10%** over the last **100** years! We often try to jump to more complex investments, but let's start with the easier ones that are proven to be effective and efficient before we jump to bigger plays. Warren Buffet, the G.O.A.T investor, says, **"I don't try to jump over the big hurdles. I simply step over the small ones."**

Next is understanding what active and passive income is. **Active income** is income that we must complete a task or action to receive payment, while **passive income** is basically getting money in our sleep! The key, she said, is to turn active income into passive income, while focusing on **multiple streams of income**.

Going through a global pandemic has proven to all of us that having **one source of income will not cut it anymore**! Over 60% of people lost their jobs or were furloughed due to COVID-19, and 74% of Americans don't have enough money saved for a $400 dollar emergency. Pairing job loss and poor savings planning is a clear recipe for disaster.

What's more stable? A table with one leg or a table with four legs? And that is the exact reason why having multiple streams of income is a must, period!

Lastly, we need to understand **compounding interest**. Interest is when your saved money earns money. Compounding interest is when you earn money on the money you saved and the money that you earned through regular interest. **The longer you have money in an investment or high-yield savings account, the better.**

We need to know that we have time on our side. By saving and investing early and often, we can take full advantage of compounding interest. Compounding interest can work for you if you save and against you if you borrow. Financially literate people invest early and often and take advantage of compounding interest, while financially illiterate people fall victim to credit cards and other forms of debt—having compounding interest work against them!

Key Takeaways:
- Take action
- Active and Passive income
- Multiple streams of income
- Compounding Interest

Chapter 8: Focus
Tyron Brackenridge
Founder, B.O.S.S. Empire

Former NFL and CFL player, entrepreneur, and most importantly to him, father: Tyron Brackenridge is such a down-to-earth person filled with tons of knowledge.

When I asked T Brack about his number-one lesson learned during COVID, he said, "Focus." He added, **"There are two types of people in this world: you are either waiting and whining or working and winning."** Makes complete sense!

During this period of stillness and unrest, we all had a choice to **learn a skill, start a business, or create a digital product that brings us money in our sleep.** Now, if you did the opposite of those things, it's okay because you have the opportunity right now to **take action**.

The hardest thing is just starting. So I would like to challenge you today to start that diet, create that budget, open that investing account! **Just get started!**

Other practical lessons and values that I took away from T Brack were: **1) Have a "financial GPS"; 2) Be aware of your subscriptions; 3) When you buy life insurance, buy the term and invest the difference.**

"How are you on the road to riches with no GPS?" was the first thing that came to my mind when T Brack mentioned it. What T Brack means by having a financial GPS is that we must have a plan that gives us some sort of direction in our personal financial situations. Life is a long journey, and if you fail to plan, then you plan to fail.

Next is being **aware of your subscriptions!** I know what you're thinking: It's only $5 dollars a month. But $5 to $10 a month from seven different subscription services will add up! This leads back to the first rule of personal finance: **You must understand what's**

coming in and what's going out. Saving on these small amounts will have a big impact on your finances over time, so be sure to check everything you are subscribed to to make sure it's essential.

Then there's number three. I could not have T Brack in this book without mentioning life insurance. Now T Brack is a heavy proponent of **term life insurance**. There are two forms of life insurance: **term** and **whole life**.

Term is a policy that covers or insures you for a certain period; whole life insurance is a policy that insures you for the entirety of your life. The other main difference between the two is that whole life carries with it a **cash value savings account**, which is invested into the stock market or another appreciating asset.

"And that's the problem with whole life", according to T Brack and other term life believers. T Brack believes in buying the less-expensive term policy and investing the difference you'll save. "Don't mix investing and insurance." T Brack says.

He advises that you **do your own research and educate yourself** on which insurance and coverage is the right choice for your personal situation, but having no life insurance is not a choice! Life insurance is key to building generational wealth for our loved ones. Period!

Key Takeaways:
- Don't wait and whine. Work and win
- Have a financial GPS
- Be aware of your subscriptions
- Buy the term life and invest the difference

Chapter 9: Peace and Options
Billionaire Billy
Stock Trader and Investor

Real deal Billionaire Bill is an options trader extraordinaire! He believes **serenity** and **peace** are huge for your **mental health**.

A lot of us are starting to take mental health more seriously, but it's still a topic that most people don't like to talk about—sort of like finances! Two conversations that are typically frowned upon in minority households: **mental health** and **money**. You know why? Because people fear what they don't understand, and those were two topics that we did not understand due to a lack of information and resources.

But I do find it funny that Billionaire Billy said that he is focused on serenity and peace because being an options trader, there probably isn't too much peace when trading. As I like to say on the show, **"Trading is more for short term profit while investing is for long term wealth building."**

So, when you compare trading and investing, trading will always be more frequent and less predictable. There are five basic types of trading out there:

Day trading is buying a stock when it's low and selling within the same day. Because remember, with almost anything in investing—stocks, real estate, trading cards, shoes, art—the goal is to always buy low and sell high!

Scalping is perhaps a little bit less known than day trading, but it's actually faster! With scalping, you are buying a stock at the bid price and selling at the ask prices. Profit margins are smaller, but they come with less risk than day trading and our next strategy.

Swing trading is very simple —in fact, the only difference between all these types of trades is the length of time you hold the security. With swing trading, you're buying a stock and usually selling it within a few weeks.

Position trading is the same as swing and day trading, but with position trading, you will be holding the contract for months or years compared to a week or two with swing - or a day or so with scalping and day trading.

Options trading is what Billionaire Billy does, which can be a bit more difficult than just buying and selling a stock. With options, you are basically betting if a stock will go up or down. You have these things called **contracts**, which are worth 100 shares, and you are essentially placing a **call** or a **put** on the stock. You place a call if you believe the stock will go up and a put if the stock will go down.

One lesson that Billionaire Billy strongly stressed was in any kind of trading—whether scalping, day, swing, position, or options trading—**DO NOT GET GREEDY!** Take your profit and go!

When Billionaire Billy trades, he likes to set profit margins so he knows what he should be gaining out of each trade. So when his margins are looking right, he's taking his profit and dipping! This lesson is especially important for young or inexperienced traders because trading is a much riskier game than long-term investing. You could be up $5,000 and lose it all in 5 seconds. But hey, that's trading for ya!

Key Takeaways:
- Serenity and Peace
- Five different types of trading
- Do not get greedy—take profit, don't lose profit!

Chapter 10: Gratitude
Sheldon Martin, aka Credit Sheldon
Credit Influencer and Finance Strategist

Another one of my Fri-end-tors- (Friend and Mentor) - who believed in me from day one. Credit Sheldon was one of the first guests on my podcast FYI FLI, and he taught me so much!

Credit Sheldon indicated that his most important lesson learned during the unprecedented time of COVID-19 was **gratitude**.

"Don't focus on what you don't have, but focus on what you do have," he told me. This quote is huge because, in life, we must be able to take what is handed to us and utilize it to its full capacity. In any situation, whether it be business, personal, leisure, sports—whatever you are doing—**we must maximize our opportunities to the fullest**. By maximizing the level you are at now, you show God that you are grateful and allow him to bless you with more.

So, I know you didn't think I was going to include Credit Sheldon in here and not give y'all game on **CREDIT**!

The number one rule that Credit Sheldon gave FYI FLI was to always, by any means necessary, pay our balances off and **pay them on time**. The biggest factor that impacts your credit score is **on-time payments**. These payments make up 35% of your entire score.

I asked Credit Sheldon how we could make these payments on time, all the time? His response to that was **automated payments**, and I could not agree with him more. **Automation is the key to setting up life-changing habits**. We should all be striving to set up automation for our payments, investing, and saving! Set up those payments and

'Fuggedaboutit' about it!

Next, be aware that you never use more than **30%** in **credit utilization**. No more than **10%** is ideal for achieving the highest score. Credit utilization is the amount of credit you've used compared to the amount of credit you have available. For example, if you have a credit limit of $1,000,

then we should never use more than $300 of that $1,000! If we go over that limit, it's imperative we pay it down because **banks and lenders want to see you use the credit line, but they don't want to see a dependence on that credit card.**

Key Takeaways:
- Gratitude
- Maximize every opportunity
- On-time payments are mandatory
- Don't use too much of your credit (under 30%)
- Automate everything!

Chapter 11: Self-Healing
Tavonia Evans
Founder of Guap Coin (CryptoCurrency)

Ms. Tavonia Evans: The world's best-kept secret. Did you know that Tavonia is the first African American woman to have her own cryptocurrency trading on foreign exchange? I know you didn't—because neither did I!

Tavonia's cryptocurrency, **Guap Coin**, is a game-changer! Its main goal is to empower, educate, and provide an economic base for underserved and financially uneducated communities.

Her greatest lesson during COVID-19 was to make time for **personal** and **mental health**. Too often, we get caught up in this incredibly fast-paced world we live in and don't take time to **debrief** and **decompress**. Tavonia's recognition of this previous issue she faced is huge because we cannot solve a problem if we don't know it exists!

As far as other lessons learned from our very own Crypto Diva, we talked about some of the basics of **cryptocurrency**. It's very important to understand these basic terms so we can have a solid foundation of knowledge to build on.

First, what is **blockchain**? It's simply a digital ledger where digital transactions occur.

Second, **cryptocurrency** allows you to be your own bank and control your personal finances.

Three, A **masternode** is what secures the blockchain or digital ledger. They verify new transactions and keep things running smoothly.

CryptoCurrency is the future of currency, so it is very important that we educate ourselves now instead of staying complacent and comfortable with what we already know. I understand learning something new can be intimidating, **but the people who have the**

most knowledge are the people who make the most money. With that being said, it would be in our best interest to learn about this new wave of digital currency.

I was telling my friend that some of the biggest companies in the world, even the US government, has approved Bitcoin. Once major companies and the government are in sync and believe in something cohesively, there's pretty much no stopping it. Cryptocurrencies are here to stay, but the real question is will you learn about them and see how you can implement them into your life, or will you turn a blind eye to the largest financial revolution in the 21st century?

Now, for a non-crypto-related lesson. Tavonia told me something that hasn't left me since we spoke. She said, "It's imperative to keep **multiple accounts. Never be left on 0".**

This is huge because this can be applied to your bank accounts as well as your crypto holdings. Having your money diversified across different accounts is always a good move. And it goes back to what I wrote earlier: Having multiple streams of income is a must, so you are never left on zero!

Key Takeaways:
- Support Guap Coin and black businesses
- Make time for mental health
- Never be left on zero

Chapter 12: Health Is Wealth
William Sweet
NFL Veteran, Investor, Entrepreneur

William Sweet III, a true advocate of change. He is not just an NFL veteran—he is an investor, entrepreneur, and much more. He is using his platform to be a vessel of change for his community of Jacksonville, Florida, where he builds houses in low-income areas around the city.

When you think of "more than an athlete," that truly describes Will Sweet, and his answer to my question about what he learned from COVID-19 fell right in line. He said, **"The biggest lesson I learned was the importance of my health."**

Before COVID-19, the world was moving at an incredible pace, and when the pandemic hit, everything slowed down almost to a halt. This downtime really allowed Will to focus and evaluate his lifestyle, choices, and decisions to find areas where he could improve. As he said, his **health** and **mental health** were two areas he chose to lock in with because you can have all the money in the world, but if you are not healthy or happy, it doesn't matter.

In our interview, Will and I talked about how the NFL's G.O.A.T., Deion Sanders, attempted to take his life. Deion "Primetime" Sanders was the greatest cornerback to walk this earth, the most entertaining football player ever, and a man of much fame and fortune. But with all that, he still wanted to end it. Why? Because inside, he wasn't happy!

Will's knowledge of investing and entrepreneurship was deep, and he dropped plenty of gems, but there was one thing that really stuck with me. **He said, "There are three types of wealth: Health, Time, Mindset."**

When we think of wealthy people, we think of the super-rich people who have everything they want. But sit and ask yourself: Do those people really have everything they want? Did they have to sacrifice their health to achieve their physical wealth? So what use was all that effort if they are not around to enjoy it?

You've heard the saying, **"health is wealth"** before. Please do not let it go over your head. Everyone has a time where they'll have to go, so do what's right and take care of yourself so you can prolong your time on this earth to see the fruits of your labor!

Speaking of time: As I wrote earlier, the true definition of **financial freedom** is having the time and the options to do whatever you want when you want. That time freedom is invaluable. Think about it. The most valuable assets are **time** and **money**. One literally controls our entire world, and the other is a non-renewable resource that can never be bought back or recreated!

Mindset stability is the third asset and a very important one. As in the Deion Sanders example, you could have everything in the world—money, fame, family—and still struggle with mental illness. It's essential to keep track of these three things because sacrificing any of them could lead to a major downfall.

Key Takeaways:
- Health is wealth
- Time is wealth
- Mindset stability is wealth

Chapter 13: Adjusting & Adapting
Herman Dolce, Jr.
CEO & Founder Bella Sloan Enterprises

Herman Dolce, Jr., aka Haitian CEO, aka the People's Champ.

Like many of the guests on my podcast, Herman has multiple businesses, but his main business is his empire, Bella Sloan Enterprises. Named after his first daughter, the business teaches thousands of people the importance of credit and business credit while showing them how to acquire business funding to build the business of their dreams.

When I tell you this guy is one of the most down-to-earth, successful entrepreneurs you will ever meet, I am not exaggerating. What makes him so compelling is his **authenticity** and **compassion**. You can tell Herman is who he says he is, and does what he says he will do. And if you don't believe him, he will gladly show you his receipts!

This is one of the takeaways we talked about, but first, let's touch on his top lesson from COVID-19: Herman did not hesitate on this question and stated simply, **"Being resilient."**

Having to pivot his entire life like all of us did was a tough task for everyone, but you never truly know how strong you are until you are tested by adversity! The adversity that Herman faced was the loss of his main sources of income from teaching in-person classes. So, Herman was forced to **adjust, learn new skills, and acquire new income streams.**

In life, there will be challenges, but we cannot let those challenges beat us. We must win, and you win by **adjusting** and **adapting**—making a plan and making a play, baby!

Some of the other lessons I learned from Haitian CEO was one I briefly mentioned above: **having proof or receipts of your business success.** These receipts can take the form of client testimonials or reviews, and they are critical for your business.

Think about it. Before you go to a new restaurant, what do you do? You check the reviews! Think about how many times you've gone somewhere or tried something because a friend gave a positive review. Exactly! Customers want to see real people with real results!

This even plays into the hottest trend in business, **influencer marketing.** It's powerful because an influencer is a person your audience already loves and trusts who is endorsing your brand. It's like a client testimonial on steroids!

Another huge gem from Herman is to **"fail forward."** I know you're thinking, "What could that even mean?" A lot of people let the fear of failure stop them from pursuing their dreams and goals. Haitian CEO says, "to fail forward means it's okay to mess up! We don't have to be so hard on ourselves. When you fail forward, you are farther than you were before you started!"

Key Takeaways:
- Be Resilient
- Have your receipts—No proof, no case!
- Fail forward!

Chapter 14: Self-Awareness
Eric Jones, aka Doctor Dapper
Founder and CEO at LFLS Shoes

The first guest of season 2, and the most energetic and passion-filled guest I've interviewed to date, Eric Jones, aka Doctor Dapper.

Eric was born in a small country town in Arkansas and went through a major tragedy, losing his mother, father, and his grandmother at an early age. Major credit to Eric, though, because he did not quit. He turned **pain** into **action** that fueled him to become the man of the house and ultimately become very successful.

After college, Eric packed all his things up and moved from Arkansas to L.A., where he started his fashion empire, LFLS Shoes. His brand even got a shoutout from Queen B (yes, Beyonce!).

Not only does Doctor Dapper have his own shoe line, but he also runs a luxury tea line, networking, and event coordinating company, and even works as a coach for other entrepreneurs who want to follow in his footsteps. During our interview, I asked him, without that big move to LA, would he have achieved the same success?

His answer was NO with the quickness! He said this because Doctor Dapper believes **if you really want to grow, it requires separation**. I understand that widening your exposure leads to expansion. So, if all Doctor Dapper knew was small-town Arkansas, his goals and ambitions would most likely never exceed that place.

When asked about the lesson that impacted him most during COVID-19, Doctor Dapper said, "I had neglected myself as an individual because I was so focused on LFLS Shoes." During the quarantine, **he had to sit back and realize that the value did not start with his company; the value started within himself**. This is why it's imperative that we invest in ourselves and constantly improve every day!

Other impactful lessons I learned from Doctor Dapper included the three keys to success—**faith, finesse, and friendship. Faith** is number one because with faith in yourself and in God, you are exactly where you need to be for his plans to be executed properly.

Finesse is next because you must be able to make a play despite the odds that may be stacked against you. Sometimes you must finesse your way into situations and rooms that originally may not have been meant for you.

Number three is **friendship**, and with it, networking. Two quotes that will never leave me: **"It's not what you know, but who you know,"** and **"Your network equals your net worth."**

Key Takeaways:
- Growth requires separation
- Self-improvement is key
- Three keys to success are faith, finesse, and friendship

Chapter 15: Control The Controllables
GloZell Green
Actress & Social Media Star

The Queen of YouTube! The OG Influencer, GloZell Green! Her natural energy is off the charts!

It's clear to see why she has been so successful, working with stars like Kevin Hart, The Rock, and Tiffany Haddish, while appearing in several movies like Trolls and Ralph Breaks The Internet.

GloZell's original claim to fame was making funny and outlandish videos on YouTube. She explained that making videos was easier and less of a hassle than going to fight for time at a local comedy club. She leveraged her early fame into a successful acting and comedy career.

GloZell, like many of us, went through hardships during this pandemic. Her biggest takeaway was understanding that worrying does not make anything better. Stress does not change the problem. **If we want change in our lives, we must put a plan in motion and make a play—simple as that.** We can't focus on things we can't control—remember, "control the controllables." We should only give our time and energy to things we can control, and if we can't, then it is a waste of our time.

Two other impactful lessons that GloZell left me with were:
1) Eliminate your weaknesses and 2) Always have products for your audience.

Many times, we try to find and build on our strengths, but we rarely find time to **identify our weaknesses and work on them**. I feel that this is due to us shying away or not wanting to live in reality. It feels easier to act like a certain weakness is not there than to address it, but **true strength is in the acknowledgement and the action that follows.**

The second lesson is huge for any entrepreneur, entertainer, or athlete: What comes with these roles are people—your fans—who genuinely believe in you and want to support you. For these people, GloZell said, always make sure you have some type of product to sell. Whether it be t-shirts, coffee mugs, backpacks, etc. Get **CREATIVE**!

I'll leave you with one bonus lesson: Never be afraid to put your ideas out there—**post your content!** You don't have to be an expert in a certain field; you just need to be a little bit more knowledgeable than one other person in this entire world. If you are, then you and your content have value.

Don't worry about likes. Just make sure to put your best foot forward and step at all times!

Key Takeaways:
- Don't complain about things you can't change
- Build up areas of weakness while reinforcing strengths
- Always have products for your audience
- Post your content!

Chapter 16: Flexibility
O'Neil Parker
Real Estate Investor, Entrepreneur, Mentor

Louisiana's finest, O'Neil Parker! It was a blessing to be able to interview this man because when I hit his age, 28, in five years, I could see myself being just like him.

O'Neil Parker is a young real estate mogul straight out of the boot (Louisiana)! He is a true example of how hard work pays off, and this is evident in the platform he has built for himself. When he was my age, he told me, he was locking in and educating himself—whether that was reading, self-improvement courses, podcasts, etc.—O'Neil was on it.

When asked about his most important lesson learned during COVID-19, he told me it was to **take what is thrown at you and make the best of it**. This really makes a lot of sense. Almost overnight, we were handed a pandemic-filled world that felt like it was at a standstill. Some people got sick, some worried themselves sick, and some people grinded themselves rich!

So, whenever you are hit with something difficult in your life, take a moment to analyze the situation and figure out the available options, be flexible, and then do what my co-host and I like to say: Make a plan and make a play, baby!

Now let's dive into some of the best takeaways I learned from speaking with the young mogul O'Neil Parker. He gave my audience and I tons of games on real estate investment. **He said there are two things young and inexperienced real estate investors do when they buy a property to flip:** They go the cheap route when it comes to repairs, and/or they hire a one-man band who believes he can fix everything.

The problem with the first option is, while it saves you money, it will cost you even more money on the back end. And for the second, hiring the correct person for the job the first time will literally save you time, money, and energy, which are three things we cannot afford to waste!

One non-real estate-related gem that our guy dropped was that **we must work hard in our 20s and 30s so we can chill in our 40s and 50s.** I couldn't agree with that more because I'm starting to see the true power of compounding in anything! Whether it be money or your consistent efforts toward something, **you will see results if you are consistent and relentless.** If you **save** and **invest** reliably, in time, you are guaranteed to see results.

You can see the biggest factor in that equation is **time**. Put in the work now, build up your own compounding interest in whatever you're doing, and watch the major progression 5 to 10 years later!

Key Takeaways:
- Hard work pays off
- Don't go cheap on real estate
- Don't go for the one-man-band in real estate
- Work hard now so we can chill later

Chapter 17: Evolve
Jully-Alma Taveras
Award-Winning, Bilingual Money Expert

My time with Jully-Alma Taveras—AKA The J.Lo of Personal Finance or better known as "The Investing Latina"—was greatly appreciated. Her passion for finance and freedom comes from growing up and watching her mother wake up and grind every single day.

For Jully's mother, the grind wasn't an option but pure necessity. "Being an immigrant In this country, my mom had to take a minimum-wage job because that's all that she could do, She had very few options." Jully told me. "That's why financial freedom is so important to me, because being financially secure allows you to live your life in the way you feel it should be lived."

That passion and determination to do better for herself and her family have led to many great accomplishments for Jully. For one, she's known as the Investing Latina and The J.Lo of Personal Finance. What's cooler than that? LOL.

But seriously, Investing Latina isn't just a cool name, Jully-Alma empowers over 7,000 learners in the LatinX community to invest and be financially secure. She has also won multiple awards, including Most Entertaining Content Creator and Best Personal Finance Creator For Underserved Communities. Jully has even spoken at the White House on the financial impact that COVID-19 has had on minority communities.

When I asked Jully about the biggest lesson she learned during COVID-19, she had a couple, but number one was the new realization that in order to thrive, you must evolve. Before COVID-19 hit in early 2020, Jully and her sister were planning a "work-cation" in Europe to relax and plan new ideas for their businesses, but then she was forced to evolve.

Although Jully lost her in-person teaching job due to COVID-19, she did not lose her hustle and passion to create freedom for herself and others. Jully began teaching investing workshops and classes and now has over 7,000 students in her program. Not only did she evolve–she got involved! She has leveraged her social media presence to become a financial influencer, creator of brand partnerships, and master of passive income deals that bring money in her sleep!

With that being said, we all have lost a lot during COVID-19, so please use Jully's story as a reminder not to focus on what you don't have, but to focus on what you do have and to build on top of that!

As far as my biggest takeaways from our interview, we have **lazy investing, panic selling, and ETF investing.**

I was so excited to speak with Jully because she is a proponent of long-term investing. I know long-term sounds so far out, especially when you are in high school or college, but as we know, **time moves fast**! For some of us, it seems like we were just in school and now we are adults trying to figure our way out in this complicated world. The way I look at it is, **if we start now by investing a comfortable amount consistently, we can almost guarantee ourselves a huge pot of money to fall back on when we're older.**

I know we all want to chase fast cash because it's more exciting and a quicker payoff, but why not set a small amount aside as your "just in case fund"? What if you don't make it as a professional athlete? What if your rapping or singing career doesn't take off? I pray it does, but if it doesn't, having money to fall back on will create that peace of mind that all of us should be attempting to obtain. **Set up automatic or automated investing and forget about it! Be a lazy investor!**

The next takeaway was something that I made sure to put in this book because normally it would make sense to sell something that's losing value right? Well in the stock market, things are a bit different. In the sense of being a long-term investor, we know that the stock market goes up and down **ALL** the time. No one actually knows **WHEN** the market will go up or down, but what we do know is that over the last 100 years, the stock market has averaged a 7% to 10% return on money invested. Since we know that a down market will rebound and go up eventually, there is usually no reason for long-term investors to sell when stocks are down or in the red. This is called **panic selling**.

Jully explains that this occurs when someone sells a stock for cheaper than they bought them because of a rapid drop in that specific stock price. Now I told you things were a bit different in the stock market. When stocks are **LOW** it's a **GO! When the market is in the red, look at it as a discount.** The stocks are now cheaper than they were, so as smart investors we take that discount and we make a play.

On the opposite end, **tons of new investors make the mistake of buying into the hype**. When a company is the center of media attention and everyone is talking about them, it's already too late. So instead of buying that stock when it was at a really low discount, you bought that stock at the highest price because your friends told you to jump in before it's too late. The blind leading the blind. In general, with anything sales or investment-related, **you always want to buy for a low price and sell for a high price.**

Now if buying, selling, and tracking stocks is too much, then no worries. Our final takeaway is the simplest way to begin investing. An **ETF** stands for an exchange-traded fund but simply think of it as a **group of stocks**. Jully likes to refer to ETFs as a "beautifully wrapped basket of stocks with a nice bow on it" and that's exactly what it is. Jully describes the gifts in this "basket" as different stocks that automatically diversify or spread out your investments. The beauty of investing in a group of stocks compared to one individual stock is if one stock in an ETF does poorly or loses value, then it's okay because you still have the other stocks in the group that are producing well.

But when you are invested in an individual stock, one bad thing could happen and your money will be dropping right along with that stock value.

Another key benefit of ETF investing is compounding interest. Compounding interest is basically earning money on the money you've already invested. So for example, let's say you invested $1,000 in an ETF that gives you a 10% yearly return. By the end of the first year, you would've earned $100 (10% of $1,000 = $100), so now you have $1100. After your second year, the $1100 has earned us $110 in compounding interest because 10% of $1100 = $110, bringing you to a total of $1,210! Now imagine that compounding over 10-20-30 years!!!

Key Takeaways:
- Evolve
- Lazy Investing
- Avoid Panic Selling
- ETF Investing

Chapter 18: The Importance of Community
Corey Paul
Rapper/Podcaster/Financial Literacy Enthusiast

The Heartbeat of Houston, my big brother, Mr. Corey Paul. One of the realest guests I interviewed, but that's to be expected: He's from H-town, Texas!

Corey Paul is a rapper, podcaster, financial literacy enthusiast, and father! CP has a podcast called the Literacy Kings that he hosts with his best friend, "J with the MBA." They break down different financial books and literature in culturally relevant, relatable, and understandable ways.

When I interviewed CP on FYI FLI, I asked him what was the biggest lesson he learned during COVID-19, and he said the **importance of community**. Like many people, Corey Paul can be an introvert at times (preferring to be by himself) and an extrovert at other times (preferring to be with people).

I, too, fall into this category. Growing up, I used to call myself an "introverted extrovert" because sometimes I like to be around others, and sometimes I want to be alone—although more often than not, I prefer to be around people.

This is what was so tough during the pandemic we all went through—the removal of in-person interaction, all athletic seasons canceled, high school proms canceled, concerts…etc. Truly a time where a sense of community was obsolete.

A supportive community can provide so many benefits for us, and not just in our social life. **The feeling of being with and accepted by a community is proven to increase your physical and mental health.** When a community is in-sync, they are more likely to be **resilient** and **adapt together**. Due to the lack of human interaction, it was very tough for most of us to adapt to the new isolated world where we were forced to live.

As far as my personal takeaways from interviewing my man, CP: One, Always **provide value**. Whatever room, Zoom meeting, or live event you're in, **you must show up, show out, and provide value!**

Providing value to your audience is the true way to bring back repeat customers, engage business partners, and even create genuine friendships.

The only way to get what you want in this world is to have leverage. If you have nothing to offer, nothing that people want, then you have no leverage. You have no bargaining power. This is why we can never stop self-improvement!

Focusing on **self-improvement** is the second biggest takeaway from CP. Legendary owner of the Miami Heat, Pat Riley says, "Complacency is the last hurdle between any team and greatness." **Being complacent or satisfied with your current position is never okay.** It's even more imperative for my former students who are no longer in school. We have to seek out information and learn new skills to continue growing and providing value!

The third takeaway was a huge one. CP said, "**You can't change the past, nor can you control the future.**" This automatically made me think about what we can do now to give ourselves a higher probability of winning in the future. As CP said, "we can't control the future, but we can put in the work now." We can educate ourselves and then take action, so when our big moment or opportunity is among us, we can make a play and execute!

Key Takeaways:
- Always provide value
- Focus on self-improvement
- "You can't change the past, nor can you control the future."

Chapter 19: Balance
Kyle King
Author and Business Coach

Kyle King. I could write an entire book on Kyle. That's how influential and impactful this brother is. Kyle has not only authored seven best-selling books, but he has also recently received the very prestigious honor of being chosen as a Forbes "30 under 30 Entrepreneur."

But this may not be his biggest accomplishment. If you were to ask Kyle, "Who are you and what do you do?" He would most likely say, "First, I am a man of God and a father," and then he would go into how he can help you write a book to create multiple streams of income for yourself.

I first came across Kyle on the Social Proof Podcast by David Shands and Donni Wiggins and immediately knew I had to shoot my shot to get him on my podcast. One thing about me, I'm always gonna attempt because **I'd rather miss and shoot again than to never have shot at all.** So with that being said, I shot, and it went in.

Kyle responded, which led me to interview him. Since then, our relationship has blossomed. Kyle is now my business coach and is helping me take my financial literacy empire FYI FLI to the top!

When I asked Kyle the infamous question of his biggest lesson learned during COVID-19, he gave me an answer that I agree with to the absolute fullest! He said, **"The biggest thing I learned was that balance is more important than success."**

During the pandemic, Kyle couldn't just drop off his son at school and go full entrepreneur mode. He had to **learn, adjust, and adapt** to being a full-time dad and full-time entrepreneur. **Kyle believes we need balance in our lives to direct our energy to the most important things like family, religion, and yourself!**

This is why I agree 100%. I believe the two most important things in life are **balance** and **priorities**.

We have to find the balance between the things that we want and need. The way that we do that is by basing our wants and needs on our priorities.

In Kyle King's case, his priorities are his faith and his son. So once Kyle satisfies those two, then he can focus on himself, his business, and other things he deems important in his life.

So what can you do right now before finishing up this book? **Figure out your priorities and align them with your direct needs, and then your wants should fall below that.**

The other takeaways I got from Kyle during our interview were straight gems. The first takeaway was, **"If you can't scale your business, you can't sell your business."** These are all facts here. If your business is not scalable, then no one will want to buy it because there is no growth potential. What it means to have a scalable business is that your company has the ability to grow and serve many more people or clients than it is currently doing now. The true way to have a scalable business is to **ensure your business has proper systems and processes set up.**

This leads us to our next gem that Kyle dropped: **"Businesses don't buy businesses—they buy systems."**

Think of McDonald's; They can literally set up shop in the hood, the suburbs, Japan, or England and still be pulling in billions annually. You know why this is possible? Because of systems! **Systems or SOP's (Standard Operating Procedures)** allow you to create a method and standardized procedures on how you want business tasks completed. This is so important because we may feel like we have to do everything as solo entrepreneurs. That may be the case in the beginning, but as you grow and as I grow, we have to start **automating, delegating and creating systems.**

By creating a good system, we can hand off certain tasks that other people can do so we can free up our own time. You should have detailed the system step-by-step, so anyone can step in and get active.

The last takeaway was: **"Leaders need to be empathetic listeners who are forward-thinking."** This was probably the biggest lesson for me because it was confirmation.

I listen to a lot of Gary Vee. If you don't know Gary Vee, look him up. He is one of the G.O.A.T. entrepreneurs, and one thing that he preaches a lot is **empathy**.

Empathy is one of the characteristics that I know I need to work on. Whether you are in a leadership role or not, you will always be working with people or be interacting with people. **People are the biggest assets in our lives,** so we must treat them that way. That means being empathetic towards their feelings and not just ours.

Now this part here, **being a forward thinker**, is essential. As the leader of your business, your team will only go as far as you can envision for them. **It's important to dream big and break boundaries.** We live in a new world and have the opportunity to do things that have never been done before. Get the right team around you. Take care of them, and they will take care of you.

Key Takeaways:
• Locate your balance and priorities
• Make a scalable business and create systems to run it
• Be an empathetic, forward-thinking leader.

Conclusion

To wrap everything up, I am so happy and proud you are taking your time to learn and educate yourself on financial literacy, investing, and entrepreneurship. I hand-picked each podcast guest with the intent of providing the most value for you. I want you to continue to grow and explore alternative learning methods, but soaking up information is not the end-all-be-all. **We actually have to put that information into action because education without application is worthless!**

There is no experience better than a hands-on experience. So, after reading this book—**go get active**! One of our most-used sayings on the show is to **"make a plan and make a play."** That's how simple life can be: **Analyze the situation, plan your moves, then execute. But remain flexible because unforeseen issues will occur!** COVID-19 taught us to expect the unexpected!

Speaking of making a play—there are two ways you can continue your education while making an impact on your financial future:

1. Below you will find the podcast episode of each chapter contributor. Please listen to the episode on any major streaming platform and be sure to hit them up for more information on their courses and/or coaching.

2. Visit www.fyifli.com and subscribe. Use our management tools. They are sure to change your life for the better.

Lastly, the pandemic of 2020–2021 has taught, brought, and taken many things from us, but we have a choice. We can take what life gives us and accept it without question, or we can take what life gives us and use that to go TAKE what we truly deserve.

No matter what, keep being a blessing and keep progressing!

Stay Safe
Stay Invested
Stay FYI FLI

FYI FLI THE PODCAST

HRTees

Make a Statement!

Order Yours Today

https://warriorstouch.shop/HRtees/shop/home

Learn, manage, and grow your finances with FYI FLI's money management tools. Our budgeting, savings, and debt eliminator tools are key to planning and priortizing your financial future.

Visit fyifli.com today.

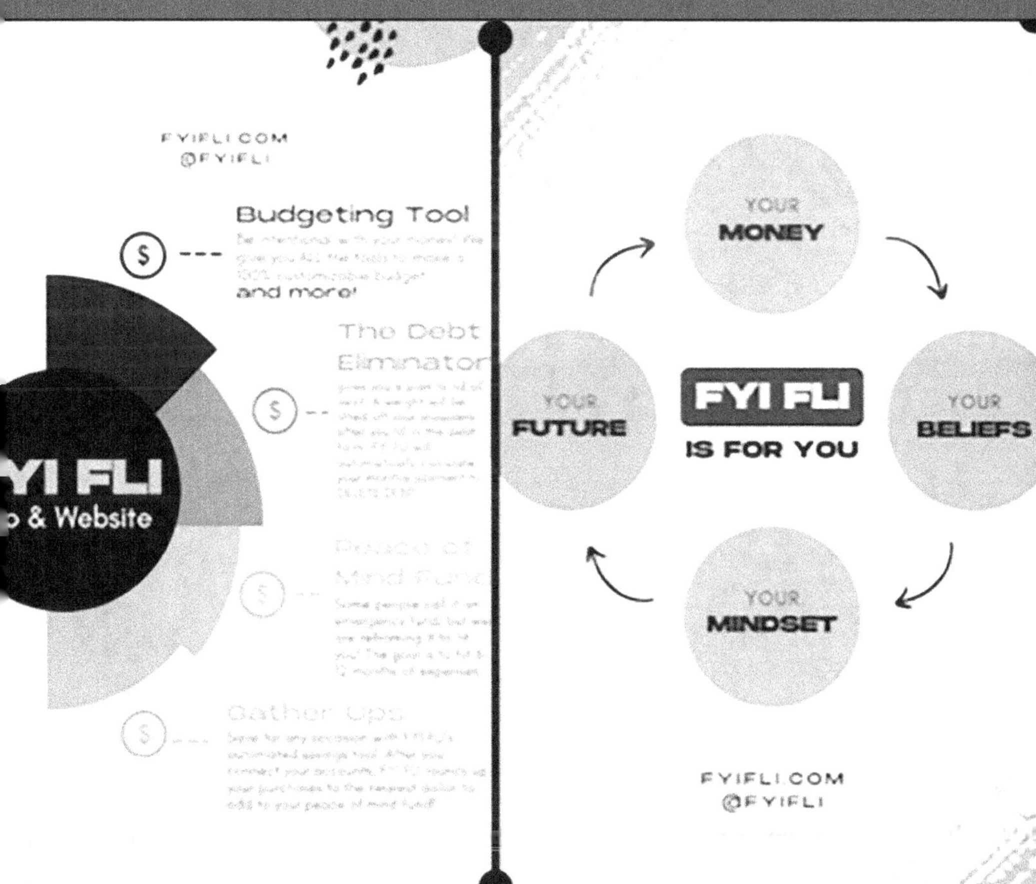

Season 1 & 2
Available on all major
streaming platforms